VOLUME 3

SING
WITH THE
CHOIR

STANDARDS

ISBN: 978-1-4234-5510-3

HAL•LEONARD®
CORPORATION

7777 W. BLUEMOUND RD. P.O. BOX 13819 MILWAUKEE, WI 53213

Visit Hal Leonard Online at
www.halleonard.com

CONTENTS

From the RKO Radio Motion Picture TOP HAT

Cheek to Cheek

Arranged by
KIRBY SHAW

**Words and Music by
IRVING BERLIN**

vil - ish like a gam - bler's luck - y streak_____ when we're out

to - geth - er danc - ing cheek to cheek._____ Oh, I

love to climb a moun - tain, and to reach the high - est peak.

But it does - n't thrill__ me half__ as much__ as

danc - ing cheek__ to cheek.__ Oh, I love to go out

*Solo 1**

Solo 2

* with Solo 2 as couple

heav - en,_____ I'm in heav - en._____

Unis.

And my heart___ beats so that I can hard - ly

speak._____ And I seem to find the hap -

- pi - ness___ I seek,_____ when we're out

to - geth - er danc - ing,_____ out to - geth - er danc -

Georgia on My Mind

Arranged by
KIRBY SHAW

Words by STUART GORRELL
Music by HOAGY CARMICHAEL

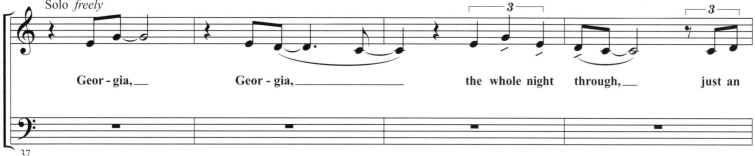

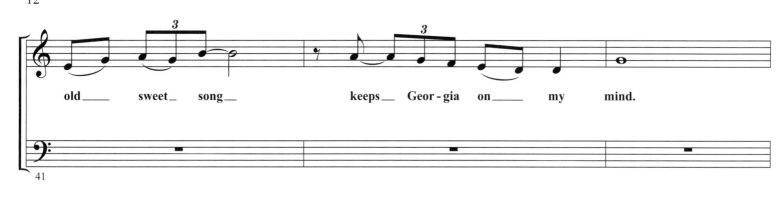

old___ sweet_ song___ keeps___ Geor-gia on___ my mind.

41

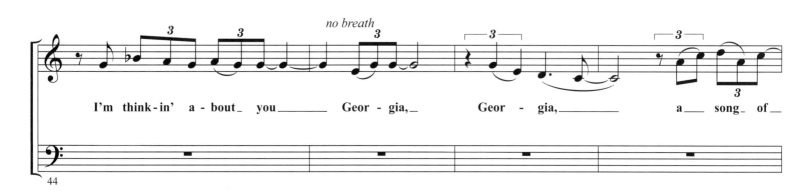

I'm think-in' a-bout_ you___ Geor-gia,_ Geor-gia,_____ a___ song_ of_

44

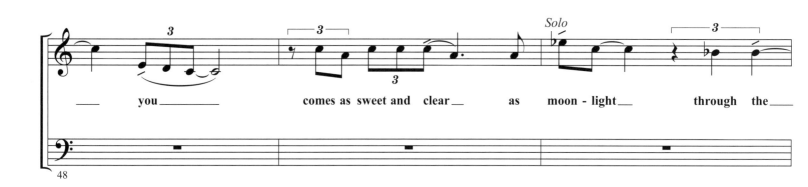

___ you_____ comes as sweet and clear__ as moon-light__ through the___

48

___ pines._____ Play it for me Geor - gia. Oth-er arms_____

51

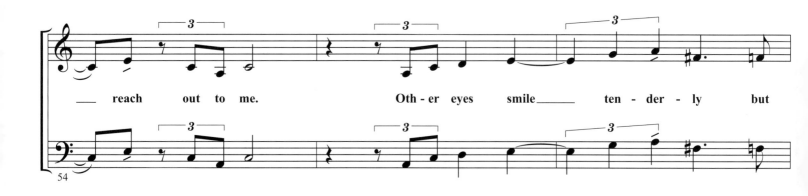

___ reach out to me. Oth-er eyes smile_____ ten-der-ly but

54

I Left My Heart in San Francisco

Arranged by
ED LOJESKI

Words by **DOUGLASS CROSS**
Music by **GEORGE CORY**

featured in SOPHISTICATED LADIES

I'm Beginning to See the Light

**Arranged by
KIRBY SHAW**

**Words and Music by DON GEORGE,
JOHNNY HODGES, DUKE ELLINGTON
and HARRY JAMES**

From the Paramount Picture BREAKFAST AT TIFFANY'S

Moon River

**Arranged by
ED LOJESKI**

**Words by JOHNNY MERCER
Music by HENRY MANCINI**

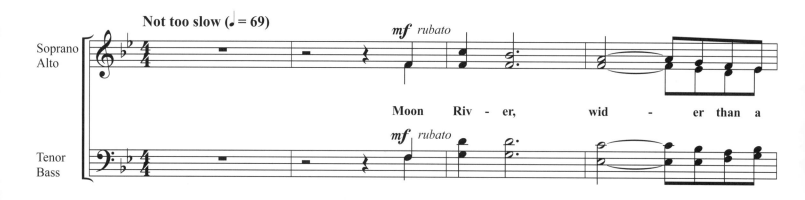

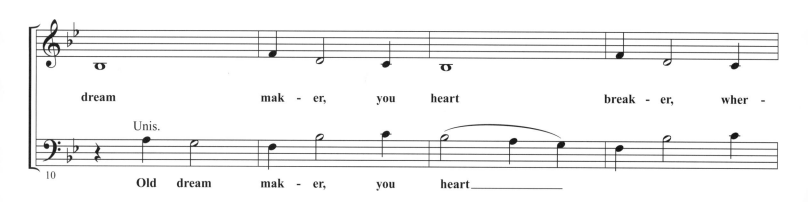

On the Sunny Side of the Street

Arranged by
MAC HUFF

Lyric by DOROTHY FIELDS
Music by JIMMY McHUGH

Skylark

Arranged by
MAC HUFF

Words by JOHNNY MERCER
Music by HOAGY CARMICHAEL

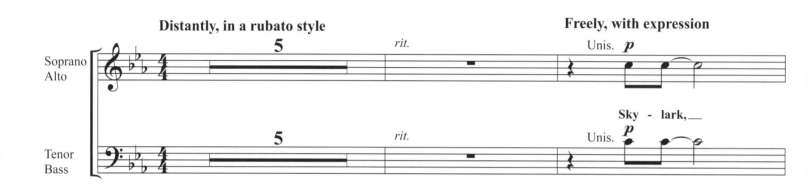

When I Fall in Love

Arranged by
MARK BRYMER

Words by EDWARD HEYMAN
Music by VICTOR YOUNG

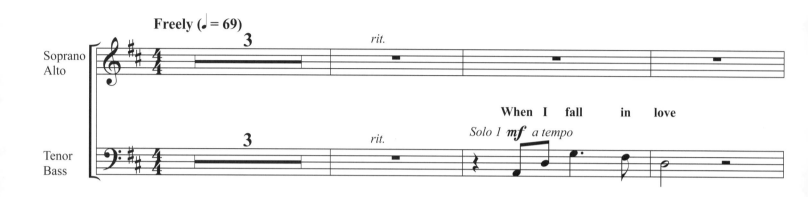

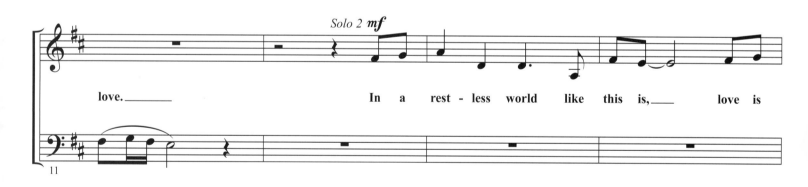

kiss - es seem to cool in the warmth of_____ the sun.

Faster (♩. = 72)

When___ I fall_____ in love_____

it_____ will be_____ for - ev - er_____

or___ I'll nev - er fall in love._____

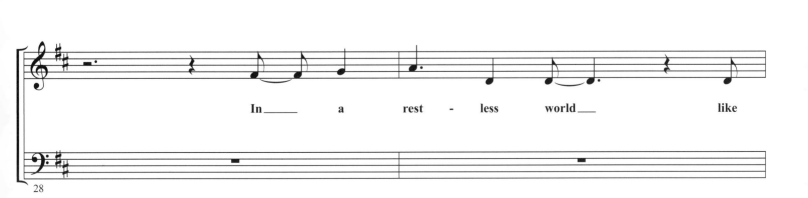

In_____ a rest - less world___ like